My
First
Book
of
Words

bluebird

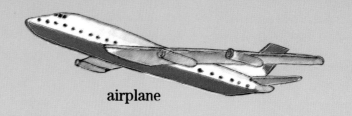
airplane

My First Book of Words

leaves

Contents

toaster

strawberry

sweater

frog

My First Bo

1,000 Words Every

boy

cat

tricycle

WORDS

ok of Words

Child Should Know

Illustrated by Lena Shiffman

wagon

girl

Cartwheel
·B·O·O·K·S· ™
SCHOLASTIC INC.
New York   Toronto   London   Auckland   Sydney

For my mother
— L.S.

ISBN 0-590-46185-0

12 11 10 9 8 7   4 5 6 7/9

Printed in the U.S.A.
First Scholastic printing, September 1992

My Body

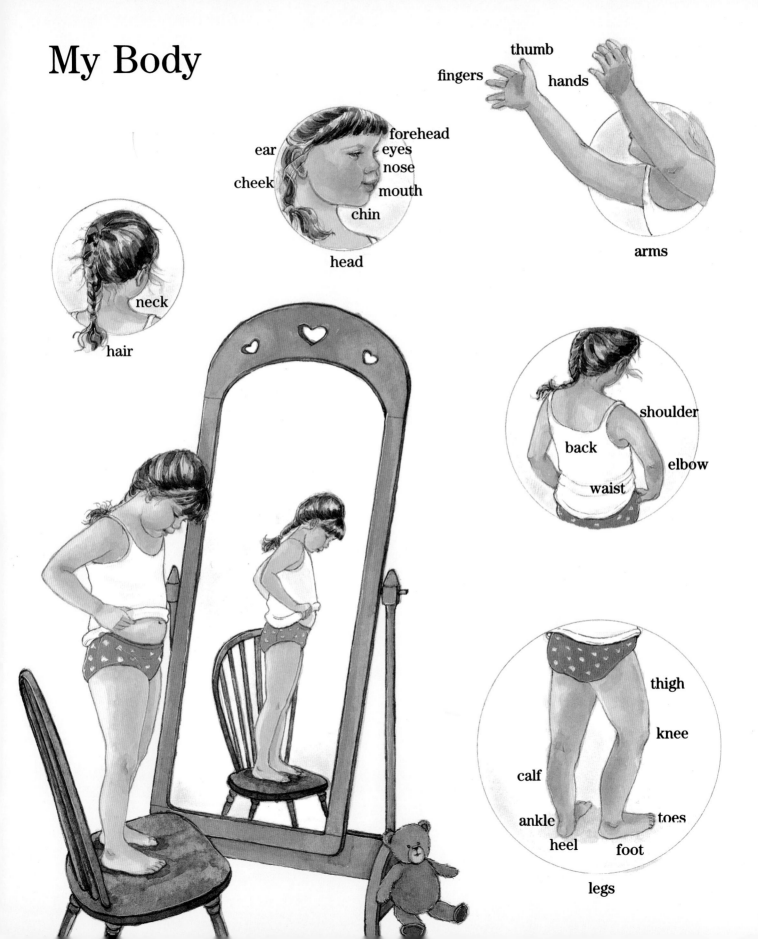

thumb

fingers

hands

forehead

ear
eyes

nose

cheek

mouth

chin

head

arms

neck

hair

shoulder

back

elbow

waist

thigh

knee

calf

ankle

toes

heel

foot

legs

My Family

grandparents

mother

me

father

sister

brother

cousins

uncle

aunt

cat

dog

My Feelings

surprised

happy

sad

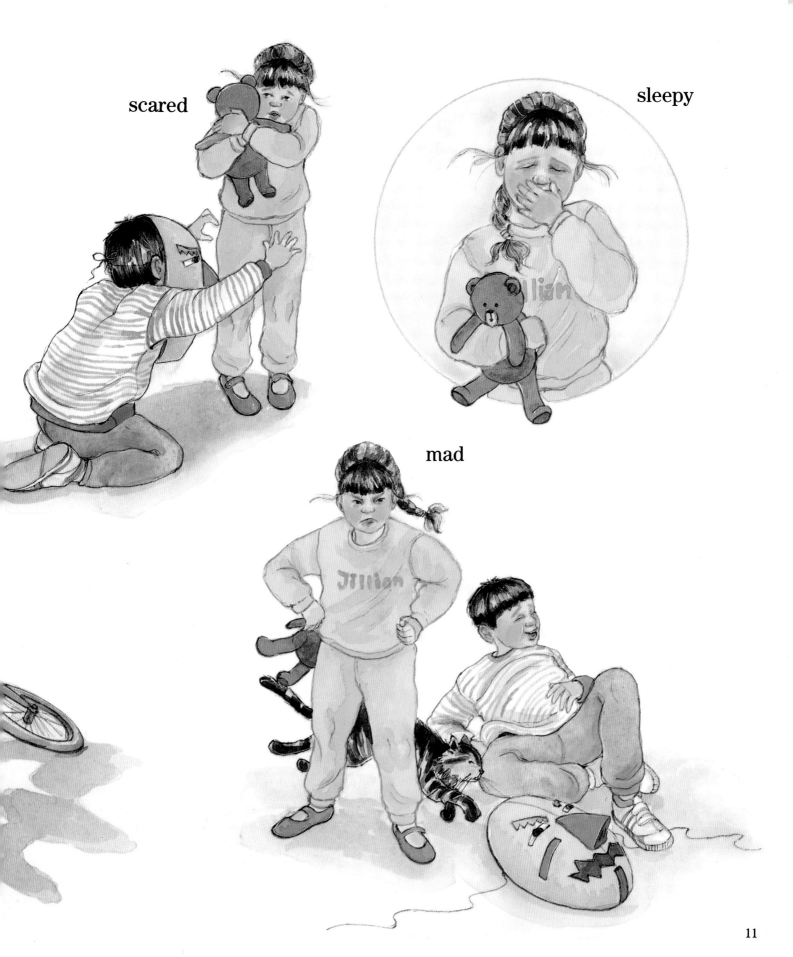

scared

sleepy

mad

11

closet

window

curtains

mirror

door

sneakers

rocking chair

dolls

dresser

drawer

bed

slippers

rug

crayons

blotter

tape

photo album

paper

puzzle

scissors

pencil holder

12

My Bedroom

books

shelf

bulletin board

pillow

teddy bear

clock

lamp

mirror

bedspread

cat

socket

nightstand

coloring book

toychest

carriage

13

My Toys

books

game

dollhouse

hand puppet

tricycle

tea set

electric train

rocking horse

teddy bear

doll

bunny

panda

ball

shovel

pail

blocks

car

truck

My Clothes

hood

nightgown

robe

diaper

pajamas

overalls

hat

mittens

snowsuit

skirt

visor

swim trunks

sneakers

bathing suit

sunglasses

sandals

T-shirt

undershirt

underpants

tank top

socks

tights

slip

shorts

shirt

aseball cap

dress

sweater

hair ribbon

tie

turtleneck

vest

belt

pants

sponge

dishwashing liquid

burner

toaster

coffee maker

canisters

glasses

vases

cups

teapot

mugs

tray

bowls

plates

cabinet

dish rack

cookbooks

glasses

faucet

sink

counter

dishwasher

garbage pail

My Kitchen

rolling pin

mixing bowl

measuring cups

wooden spoon

can opener

ladle

spatula

lid

saucepan

pot

skillet

salt and pepper shakers

microwave oven

pot holders

kettle

stove

oven

knobs

freezer

refrigerator

food

table

pitcher

cup

saucer

bowl

tablecloth

chair

high chair

cookie cutters

cookie tray

napkin

spoon

knife

fork

My Food

pancakes

syrup

milk

apple

waffles

cereal

jam

cocoa

egg

mustar

green beans

butter

orange juice

toast

Breakfast

chicken

18

carrot

grapes

Lunch

orange

chips

cookies

celery

cheese sandwich

salad

salad dressing

pickles

pepper

hamburger

baked potato

peas

soup

roast beef

Dinner

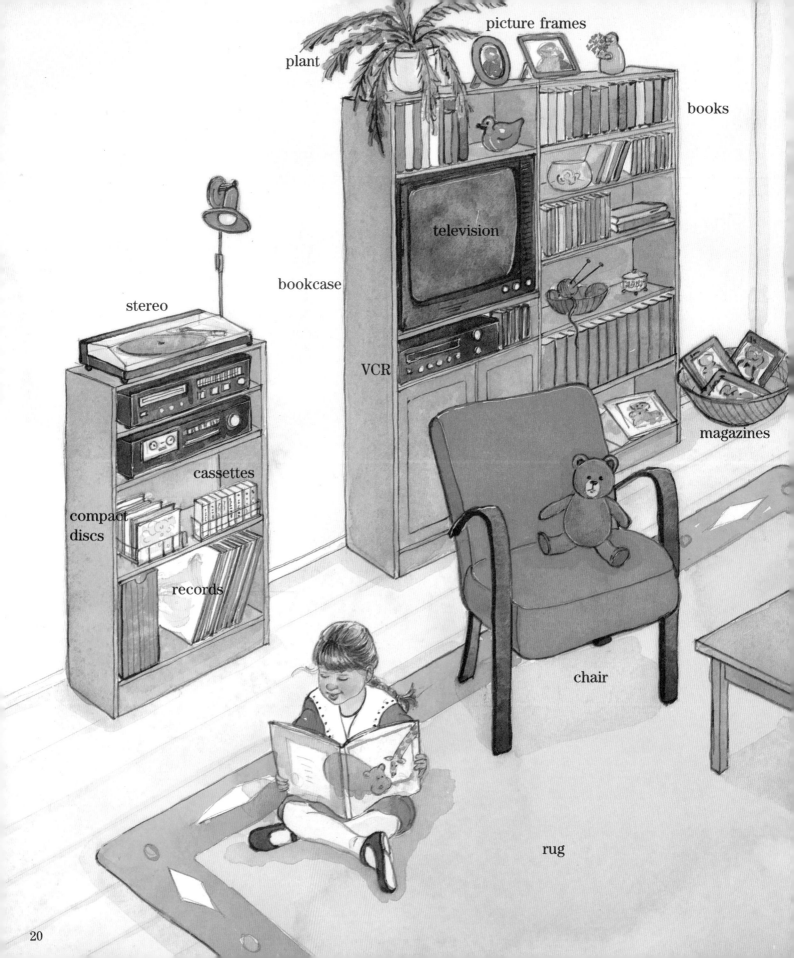

plant

picture frames

books

television

bookcase

stereo

VCR

cassettes

compact discs

records

magazines

chair

rug

My Living Room

lamp

paintings

sofa

pillows

vase

telephone

end table

coffee table

shower

faucet

shampoo

towel rack

towels

toilet paper

bubbles

bathtub

potty

toilet

shower curtain

rubber duck

tub toys

bath mat

My Bathroom

medicine cabinet

mirror

mouthwash

toothbrush

soap dish

soap

washcloth

brush

water

sink

toothpaste

laundry

step stool

hamper

umbrella

chair

table

window box

patio

door

rabbit hutch

barbecue

tree

birds

bird feeder

dog

squirrel

flowers

watering can

roses

basket

peaches

24

My Backyard

fence

doghouse

grass

wheelbarrow

thermometer

leaves

rake

garden

rabbit

bone

dish

charcoal

lawn mower

25

clock

sink

lunch pail

wastebasket

artwork

cubbies

easel

floor puzzle

My Classroom

books

mat

paint

paintbrushes

bookcase

teacher

table

chair

goldfish

fishbowl

hamster cage

hamster

backpack

paper

crayons

modeling clay

I Learn Colors

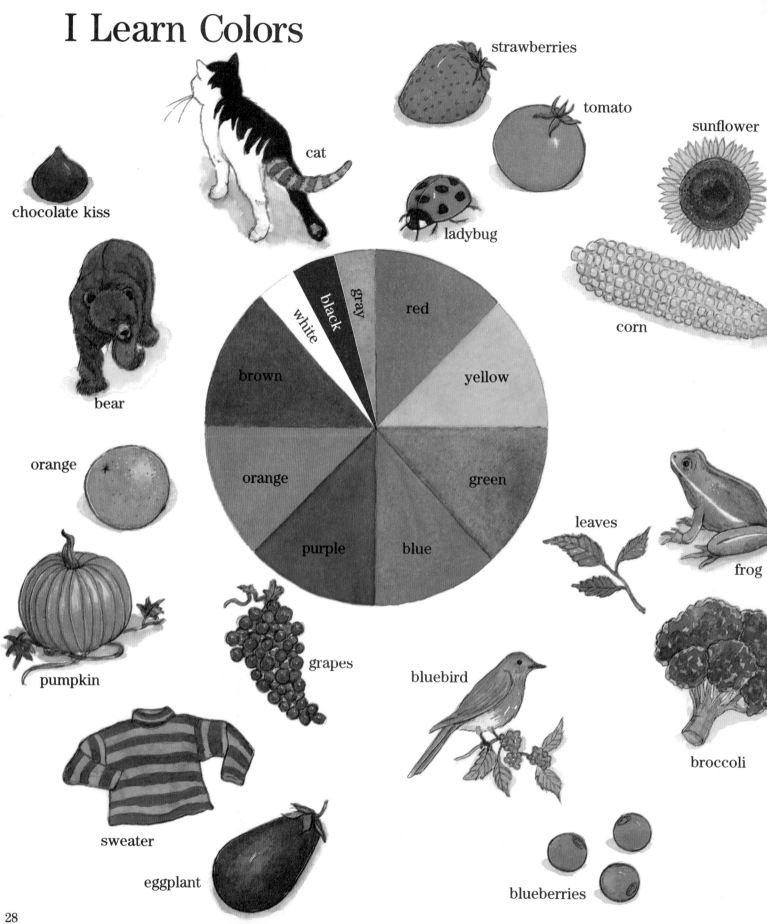

strawberries

tomato

sunflower

cat

ladybug

chocolate kiss

corn

bear

orange

leaves

frog

pumpkin

grapes

bluebird

broccoli

sweater

eggplant

blueberries

gray

black

white

red

brown

yellow

orange

green

purple

blue

I Learn Shapes

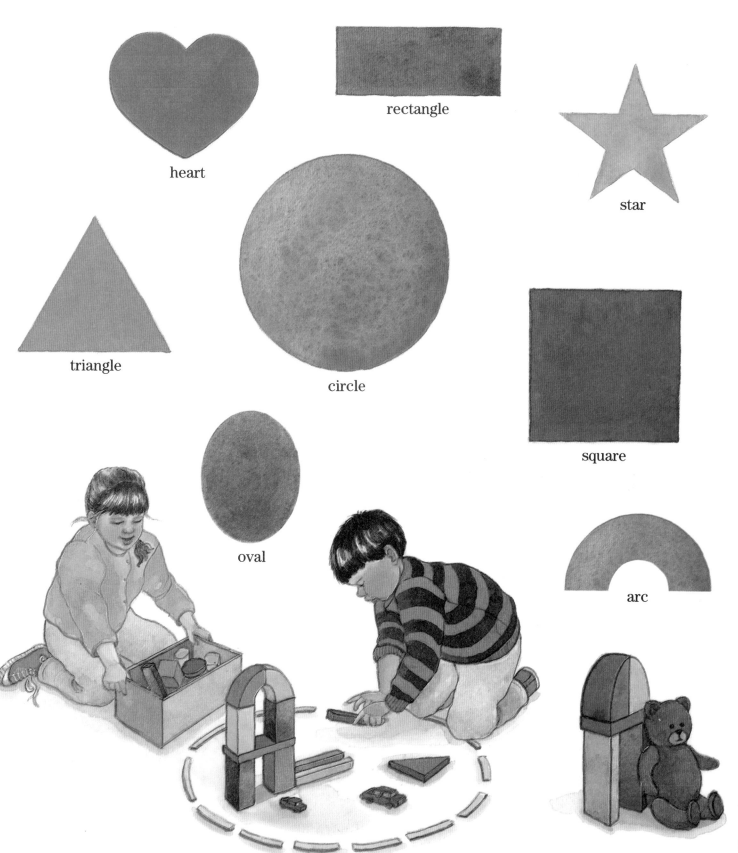

heart

rectangle

star

triangle

circle

square

oval

arc

I Learn Numbers

1 caterpillar

2 kittens

3 tricycles

4 toy cars

5 bears

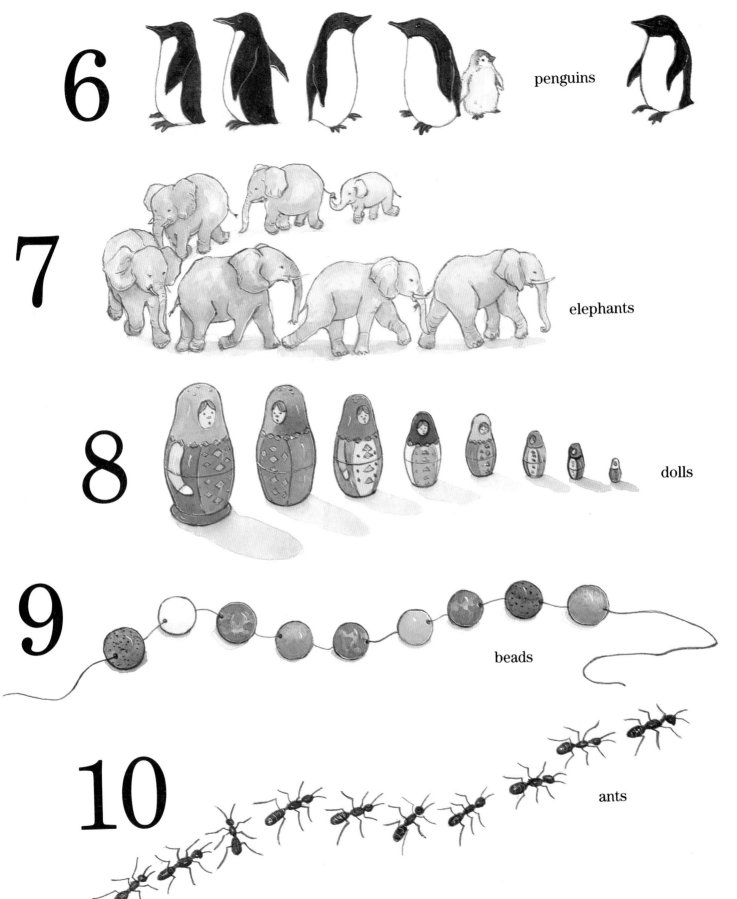

6 penguins

7 elephants

8 dolls

9 beads

10 ants

I Learn Letters

alligator

A

balloon

B

cat

C

dinosaur

D

hat

H

ice cream

I

jack-in-the-box

J

owl

O

pencil

P

queen

Q

umbrella

U

vase

V

whistle

W

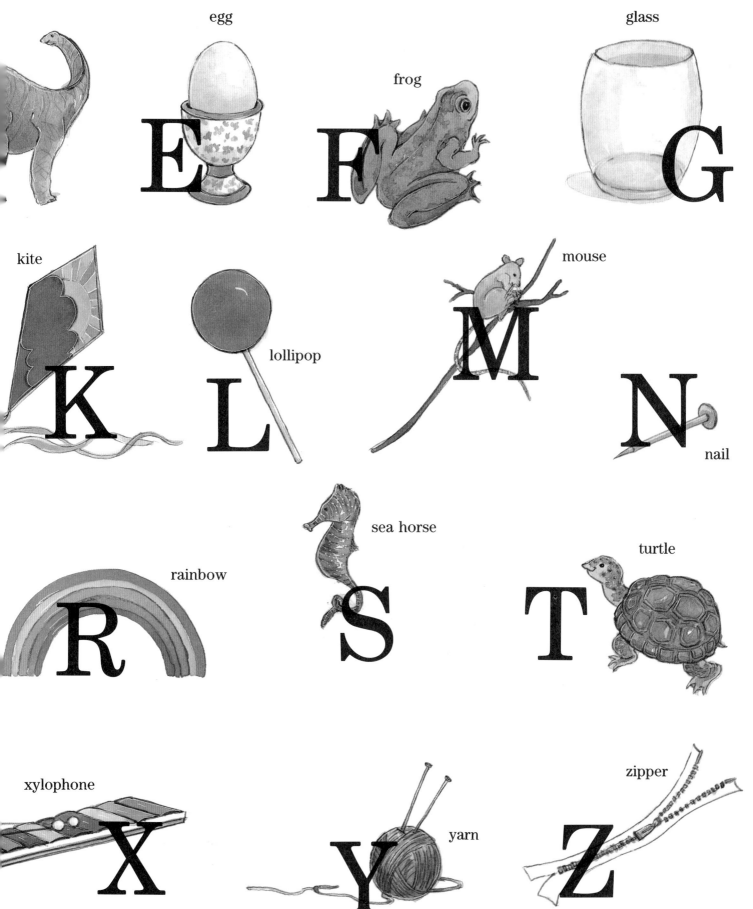

egg

glass

frog

E

F

G

kite

mouse

K

L

M

N

lollipop

nail

sea horse

turtle

rainbow

R

S

T

xylophone

zipper

X

Y

Z

yarn

harp

chimes

piano

xylophone

bat

sheet music

saxophone

music stand

trumpe

viola

violin

drum

cello

Musical Instruments

flute

piccolo

guitar

harmonica

conductor

bassoon

clarinet

tuba

oboe

cymbals

trombone

triangle

paper cups

plastic spoons

plastic forks

paper plates

party horn

favor bag

napkins

table

tablecloth

juice

cupcakes

pretzels

potato chips

party hats

My Birthday Party

streamers

balloons

presents

birthday girl

pin-the-tail-on-the-donkey

ice cream

bowls

candles

birthday cake

birthday cards

My Town

construction site

construction worker

HOTEL

Joe's Grocery

benches

fountain

grocer

traffic light

garbage truck

tree

BAKERY

baker

waiter

sanitation worker

sidewalk

garbage cans

39

soccer ball

goal

kicking

digging

swings

sandbox

swinging

laughing

running

walking

seesaw

My Playground

baseball

baseball bat

throwing

basketball
hoop

basketball

climbing

jumping

crawling

jungle gym

hanging

sliding

sitting

41

beans

corn

cucumber

mushrooms

onion

paper bag

cash register

money

DAIRY PRODUCTS

FROZEN FOODS

cheese

eggs

butter

milk

BREAD

PASTAS

COOKIES

spaghetti

cookies

bread

jam

Cereal

cereal

shopper

BANANAS

APPLES

bubble gum
machine

cashier

Cereal

coupon

SAVE 50¢

scale

42

MEATS

Fish

Deli
Ham $5.99

cauliflower

sausage

steak

salami

bacon

carrot

fish

butcher

cart

meat

MELONS

VEGETABLES

LETTUCE

WATERMELON

watermelons

tomatoes

potatoes

POTATOES

onions

ONIONS

grapes

My Supermarket

strawberries

blueberries

cherries

limes

lemon

My Doctor's Office

Waiting Room

couch

nurse

chart

plant

lollipop

books

magazines

table

blocks

stool

toy truck

tongue depressor

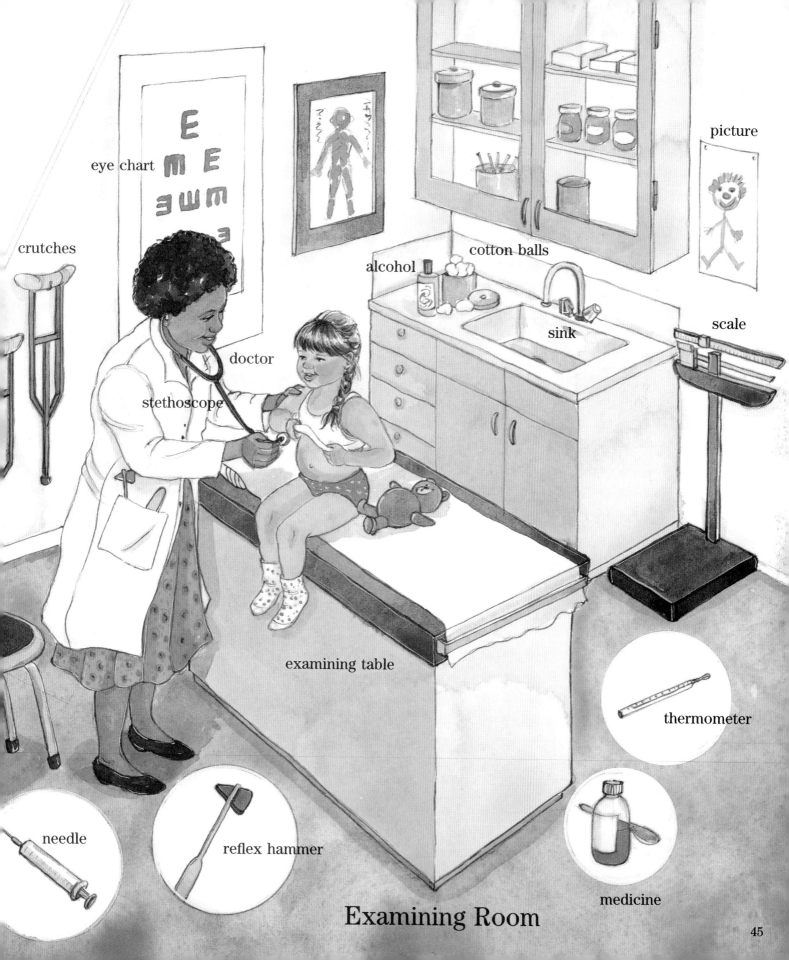

eye chart

picture

crutches

cotton balls

alcohol

doctor

sink

scale

stethoscope

examining table

thermometer

needle

reflex hammer

medicine

Examining Room

45

Vehicles

airplane

LAND

tractor

train

police car

car

trailer

school bus

truck

ambulance

camper

bulldozer

motorcycle

SKY

helicopter

freighter

storage tanks

barge

tugboat

garbage
truck

fire engine

taxi

sail

rowboat

oar

bicycle

sailboat

canoe

houseboat

motorboat

tricycle

WATER

47

Tools

plane

nuts

bolts

file

ruler

pliers

wrench

sandpaper

drill

nails

screws

hammer

saw

screwdriver

toolbox

shovel

49

Holidays

Halloween

witch

trick-or-treaters

jack-o'-lantern

ghost

candy

Thanksgiving

turkey

cranberries

Hanukkah

candles

menorah

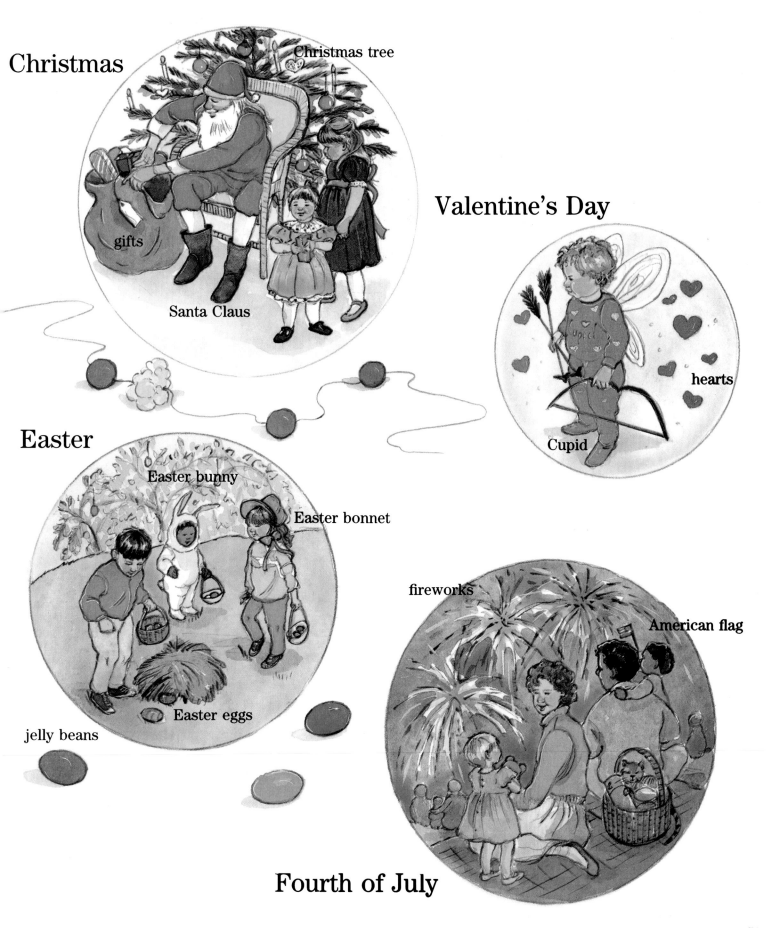

Christmas

Christmas tree

gifts

Santa Claus

Valentine's Day

hearts

Cupid

Easter

Easter bunny

Easter bonnet

Easter eggs

jelly beans

fireworks

American flag

Fourth of July

Seasons

Spring

kite

blue jay

blossoms

rosebud

robin

bird's nest

tulip

flowers

daffodil

Summer

beach ball

swimmer

pool

mosquito

bathing suit

bicycle

shorts

lemonade

sunglasses

iced tea

sandals

suntan lotion

skateboard

Fall

tree

apples

rake

leaves

pumpkin

Winter

snow

hat

frozen pond

snowman

scarf

ice skates

ski poles

mittens

icicles

snowball

skis

sled

boots

53

Weather

rain

raindrops

hailstones

wind

snowflakes

snowman

toboggan

snow

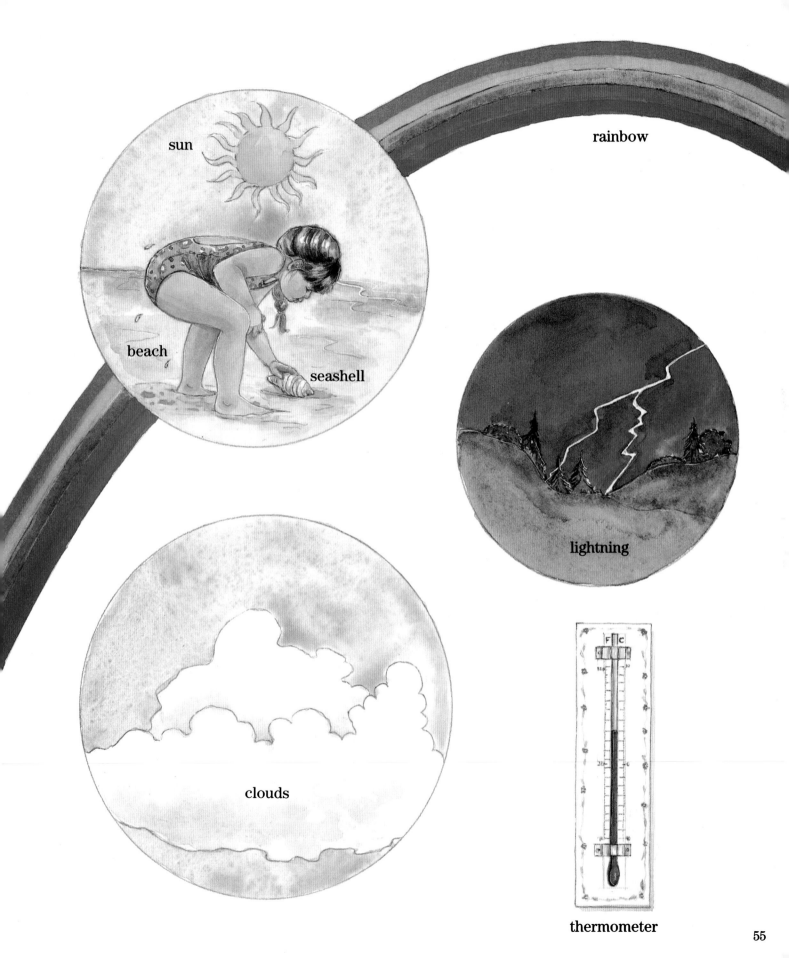

sun

rainbow

beach

seashell

lightning

clouds

thermometer

55

rooster

pig

cat

hen

chicks

kittens

goat

cow

lamb

mouse

56

silo

barn

ducks

dog

horse

Farm Animals

Zoo Animals

tiger

hippopotamus

chimpanzee

rhinoceros

elephant

giraffe

zebra

bear

camel

polar bear

penguins

sea lion

seal pup

leopard

lions

panda

Underwater Animals

whale

fish

shark

seaweed

fish

sunken ship

octopus

shrimp

coral

treasure chest

lobster

starfish

seashells

horseshoe crab

crab

Nighttime Animals

spider

firefly

bat

cricket

nightingale

owl

Good Night

window shade

moon

shelf

night-light

bed

teddy bear

blanket

Mommy

children

dog

bottle